This book belongs to:

....

AHLAN KIDS

Copyright © 2022 Ahlan Kids Education Ltd.

Suite 5, 29 Castle Street Kingston upon Thames, KT1 1DN, UK.

Text - Ahlan Kids Education Ltd.
Illustrations - Zahraa Akoob

All rights reserved. No part of this publication may be reproduced, stored in a retrieval system, or transmitted in any form or by any means, electronic, mechanical, photocopying, recording or otherwise, without the prior permission of the copyright owner.

www.ahlankids.com

Prophet Yunus
and the whale

AHLAN KIDS

A long time ago, there was a king who lived with his people in the city of Nineveh.

They didn't worship Allah.

The people were doing bad things like stealing, lying, cheating, bullying, betraying others, gossiping and worshipping idols.

Almighty Allah sent Prophet Yunus to teach them to do good actions and to worship Allah.

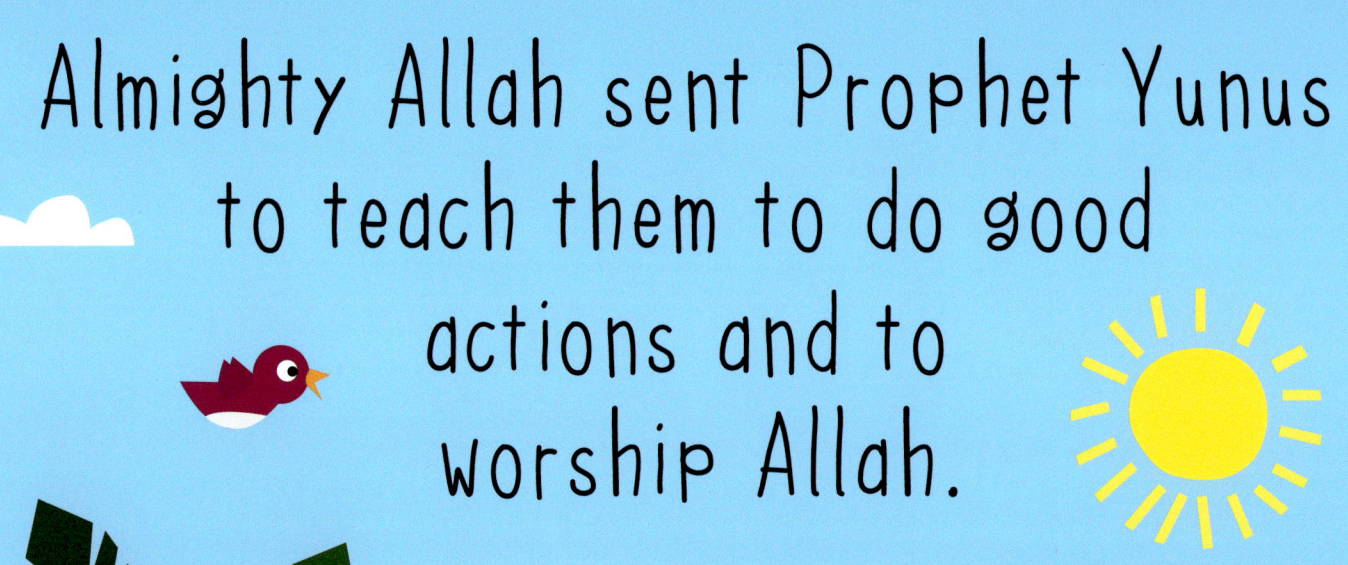

"There is only one God."

He spent a long time inviting people to the path of Allah but only a few people followed his message.

Prophet Yunus was angry and frustrated. He was afraid something bad was going to happen to the people.

I give up! I'm done with these people!

Without Allah's permission he abandoned his mission, boarded a ship and sailed away.

Far Away....Noon the whale was swimming happily in the deep, blue sea when he spotted a boat in the distance.

Soon it became dark and stormy.

CLAP!

BOOM!

Noon was a little scared when he heard thunder.

Suddenly, he saw a man falling overboard!

"Wooooaaahh!"

splash!

Allah commanded him to keep the man, Prophet Yunus, in his belly.

Noon jumped in the air, opened his great, big mouth and... "Gulp." He swallowed Prophet Yunus!

Inside the whale's belly,
in darkness and despair,
Prophet Yunus asked himself,

"What have I done?"

Noon heard Prophet Yunus pray to Allah

"There is no God but You, you are glorious, I am one of the wrong doers."

La illaha illa Anta, Subhanaka, Inni kuntu minadhalimeen

THE DUA OF PROPHET YUNUS
(Surah Al Anbiya, 21:87)

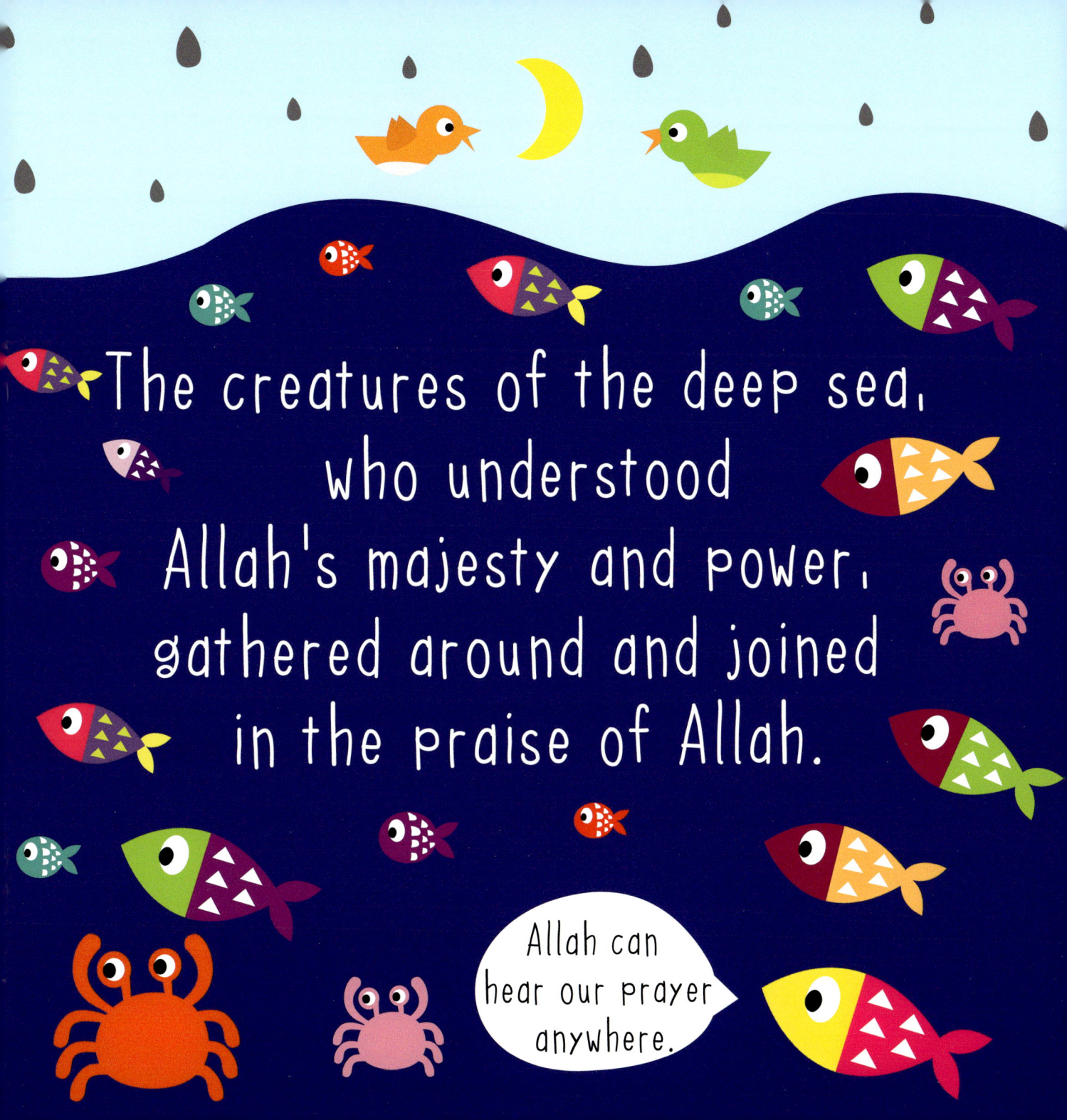

The creatures of the deep sea, who understood Allah's majesty and power, gathered around and joined in the praise of Allah.

Allah can hear our prayer anywhere.

Allah accepted his sincere repentance and commanded Noon to take Prophet Yunus to the sea shore.

Allah is Al-Ghafoor, The Most Forgiving.

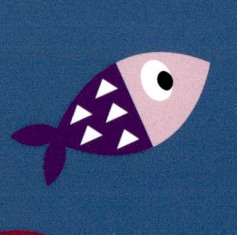

He spat him out onto the shore.

Prophet Yunus woke up and found himself

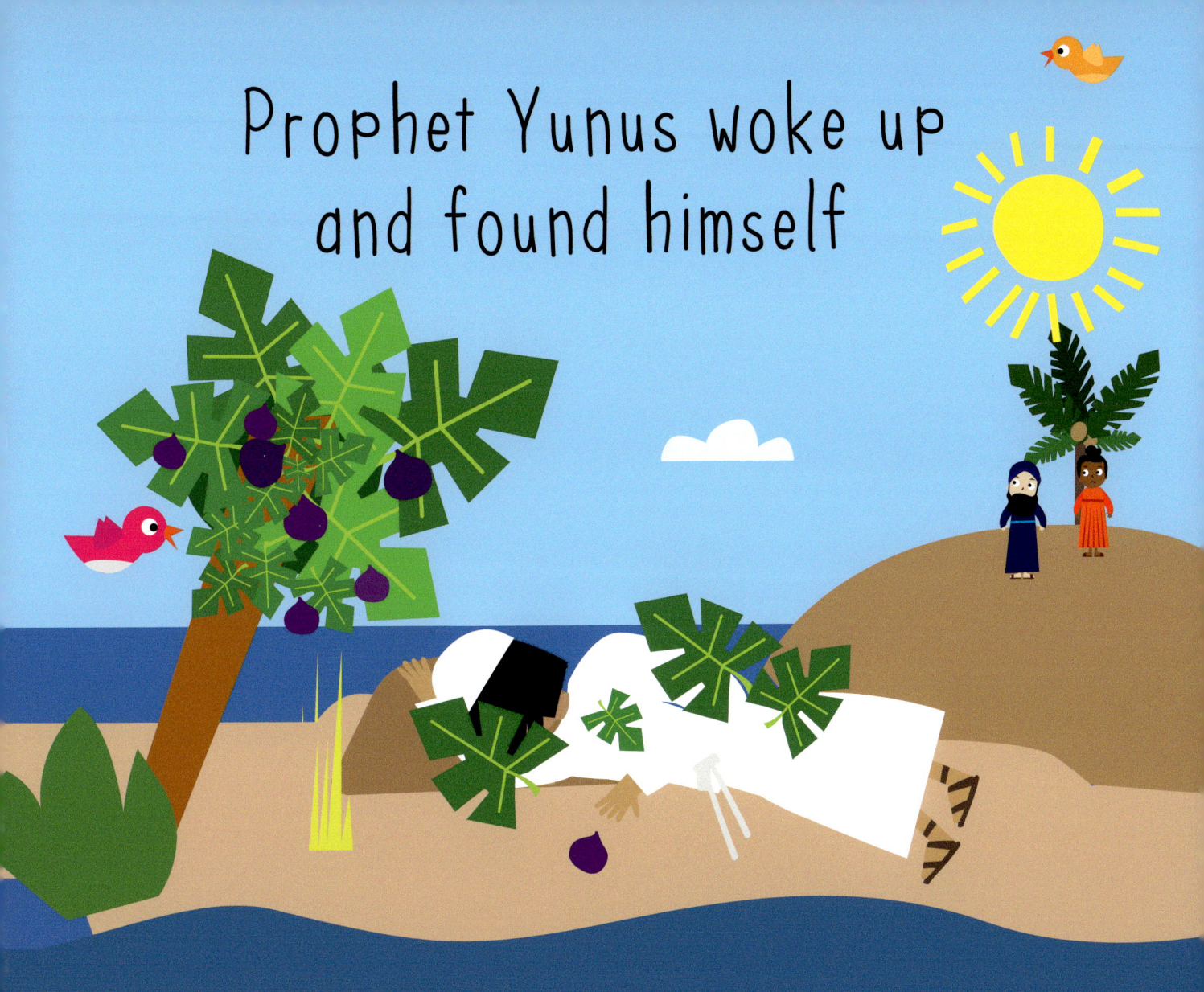

under the shade of a fig tree, protected from the scorching sun.

When Prophet Yunus returned to Nineveh he was suprised to find his people had all accepted the message of Allah!

During the great storm, one of Prophet Yunus's followers had taught the people his message.

O Allah, our sins are great, but you are greater, forgive us.

"Thank you Allah,
for saving this city and its people."

Prophet Yunus and the people of Nineveh prayed together and thanked Allah for all their blessings.